IN THE FOOTSTEPS OF MOSES

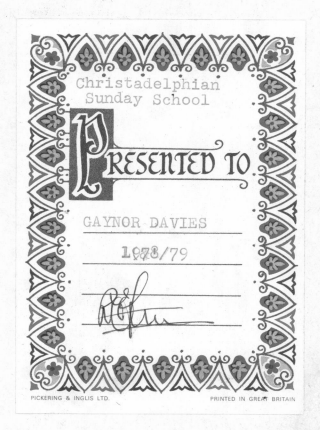

IN THE FOOTSTEPS OF MOSES

OLIPHANTS
LONDON

MOSHE PEARLMAN

PHOTOGRAPHY BY DAVID HARRIS

GENERAL EDITOR MORDECAI RAANAN
DESIGN CONSULTANT GAD ULMAN

OLIPHANTS
116 Baker Street
London WIM 2BB

First British Paperback Edition 1976

Published in:

Israel, by Nateev and Steimatzky, Tel-Aviv
United States of America, by Nateev
Switzerland, by Walter Verlag, Olten und Freiburg im Breisgau
France, by Edition Arthaud, Paris et Grenoble
Italy, by Coines Edizioni spa, Roma
Brazil, by Bloch Editores, Rio de Janeiro

ISBN 0 551 00757 5

ACKNOWLEDGMENTS and thanks are due to the following institutions and persons for having kindly permitted their exhibits to
be photographed: Department of Antiquities and Museums, Ministry of Education and Culture, Jerusalem; Rockefeller Museum,
pages 21, 130–31, 177; Israel Meuseum, pages 122, 184, 198; The Jewish National and University Library, Jerusalem, pages 152–53;
The Library of St. Thoros, The Armenian Orthodox Patriarchate, Jerusalem, pages 64, 72, 116; U.S. Information Service, The
Embassy of the U.S.A., Tel Aviv, page 69; The Pierpont Morgan Library, New York, N.Y., pages 181, 201; E.M. Cross, Jr., Harvard
University, pages 126–127. Photographs by Uzi Paz, page 104; by Werner Braun, page 106; by other photographers, pages 13, 14–15,
25, 26–27, 125, 128.

Printed in Israel by Peli Printing Works Ltd.

CONTENTS

AUTHOR'S NOTE

I thank Dr. Moshe Weinfeld, Senior Lecturer in Bible, Hebrew University,
Jerusalem, who read the manuscript and made valuable suggestions, particularly
on the covenant tradition in the ancient Near East dealt with in Chapter 3.
My thanks go also to Magen Broshi, Curator of the Shrine of the Book,
Israel Museum, Jerusalem, and to Ze'ev Yeivin, of the Israel government's
Department of Antiquities, for their help in the selection of the illustrations.

Jerusalem, January 1973   Moshe Pearlman

A momentous event occurred some thirty-two hundred years ago which was to affect the course of history for many peoples to this very day. This was the Exodus from Egypt of the Israelites and their conquest and settlement of the Promised Land.

In this grand human adventure, the name of one man, Moses, stands out as leader, commander and law-giver. The impact of the Exodus upon the lives of a great portion of the human race lay in its spiritual message, and also in its vital political consequences. Since those days, the Law of Moses and the Land of Israel became one inseparable entity, and the hallmark of the Jewish people.

Moshe Pearlman has succeeded in giving the general reader a clear and comprehensive account of this drama, where the professional historian, archaeologist or biblical scholar, in the absence of the complete historical facts, might well have been caught in the thickets of conflicting theories and his own biased views.

The author is not a newcomer to the historical and archaeological subjects of the biblical world. His books on the historical sites of Israel and on Jerusalem are still the most readable and accurate of their kind.

"In the Footsteps of Moses" is a fascinating narrative, beautifully illustrated, which offers the general reader the gist of the history of the Jewish people in their formative years.

Yigael Yadin
Professor of Archaeology
January 1973   Hebrew University of Jerusalem